Full of Sh*t

Full of Sh*t

A Pictogram Book

By Brian Lee

ISBN: 9798341458062

Testimonials

"A crappy masterpiece, this book proves that a picture really is worth a thousand turds!" – Dave Sch(m)itt

"This book will shake you to your bowels and move you with its wit, humor, and depth. Pinch one before they sell out!" – Dr. Rick Tum, MD

"It's been a wonderful year for literature and omnilegents. With an explosion of microgenres and new authors, the competition for eyeballs is fierce, and while this book may not be at the very top of my list, I can honestly say it's a solid #2." –Sherman Pooh

Table of Contents

1. Introduction

Do you know your sh*t?

Each page has a pictogram with a number below it. Think of each pictogram as a modern version of Neanderthal cave paintings.

Guess the colloquialism represented by the pictogram.

To see if you are correct, look up the number in **This is the Sh*t!** on page 63. The solutions are also on our website, www.fullofshitbook.com. Or, scan this QR Code to have the solutions in hand.

2. What is this sh*t?

Are you ready?

#24

#37

#20

#23

#5

#40

#33

#26

#54

#12

#16

#28

#15

#51

#45

#1

#39

#46

#3

#35

#11

#6

#47

You Are Here

#32

#9

#53

#42

#8

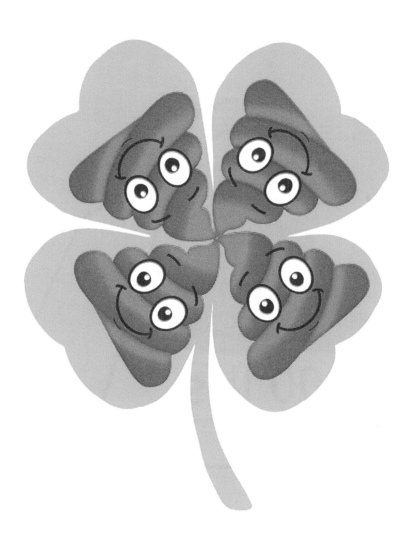

#43

2000 lbs

#14

#44

#18

#49

#29

#38

#17

#4

#19

#31

#27

#52

#48

#21

#13

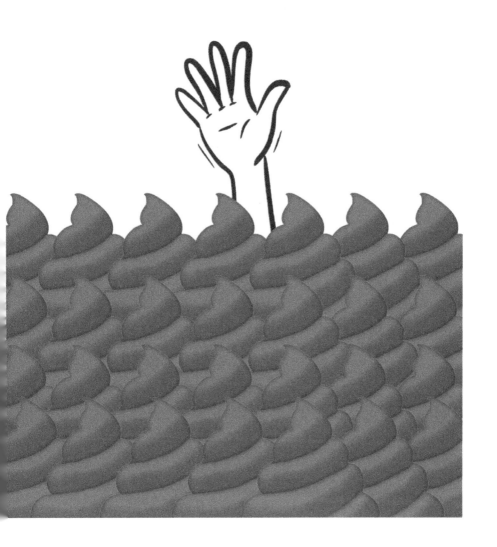

#30

#10

#7

#2

#22

#50

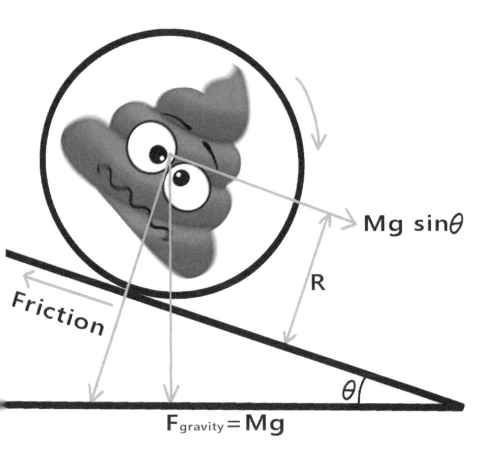

Mg sinθ

R

Friction

$F_{gravity} = Mg$

θ

#25

#36

#41

#34

3. This is the Sh*t!

1 "Bat sh*t crazy"

2 "No sh*t sherlock"

3 "Like a pig in sh*t"

4 "Starting sh*t"

5 "Cool sh*t"

6 "Sh*t for brains" or "Sh*thead"

7 "Sh*t house"

8 "Scared the sh*t out of me"

9 "Give a sh*t"

10 "Feel like sh*t" or "Sick as sh*t"

11 "Sh*thole"

12 "Chicken sh*t"

13 "Get your sh*t together"

14 "Sh*t ton", "Ton of sh*t", "Heavy sh*t"

15 "Stirring up Sh*t"

16 "Same sh*t, different day"

17 "Crock of sh*t"

18 "Sack of sh*t"

19 "Oh sh*t"

20 "Sh*t show"

21 "Catching sh*t"

22 "Got sh*t to do"

23 "Sh*t is going down"

24 "Bullsh*t"

25 "Sh*t rolls downhill"

26 "Holy sh*t"

27 "Talking sh*t"

28 "Dumb sh*t"

29 "Sh*t faced"

30 "In deep sh*t"

31 "Sh*t magnet"

32 "Sh*t list"

33 "Cut the sh*t", "Cut that sh*t out"

34 "Sh*t storm"

35 "Cheap sh*t"

36 "Tough sh*t"

37 "Sh*t hits the fan"

38 "Up sh*t creek"

39 "Piece of sh*t"

40 "Look like sh*t"

41 "Tastes like sh*t"

42 "Bad sh*t"

43 "Sh*tty luck", "Lucky sh*t"

44 "No sh*t"

45 "Hot sh*t"

46 "Sh*t canned"

47 "Eat sh*t and die"

48 "Good sh*t"

49 "Jack sh*t"

50 "Sh*t kickers"

51 "Shoot the sh*t"

52 "Dip sh*t"

53 "Crazy sh*t"

54 "Sh*t load", "Load of sh*t"

Made in the USA
Las Vegas, NV
18 October 2024